IE Survival Guide
Standard I

Organization of Dots
Orientation in Space I
Comparisons
Analytic Perception

Dr. Lynn Brown

This book is dedicated to my family and friends who encouraged me to learn and push my own thinking so that I may have a significant impact on others.

It is also dedicated to my colleagues who believe in the malleability of the human brain and that thinking should be explicitly taught instead of just caught.

Copyright © 2012 by Frameworks, LLC. All rights reserved.
ISBN 978-0-9884091-0-1

Table of Contents

Overview..4

Organization of Dots 6

Orientation in Space I..31

Comparisons 45

Analytic Perception..62

IE Survival Guide
Standard I
Overview

This booklet is an unauthorized guide and in no way supplants the Instrumental Enrichment Teacher's Guide. Instead, it is intended to be a help to the classroom teacher during their first year of implementation. These are my observations and experiences from my first year of teaching IE with helpful input from a teacher colleague. Each instrument begins with an introduction of the overall goal(s) of the instrument, followed by possible ways to teach the cover page, then aids for teaching each page. The aids for specific pages are divided into three parts:

1. Things to Consider – important ideas/concepts on each page.
2. Work on the Sheet – some possible ways to introduce the page and discussions you may want to have as you work with students.
3. Closure - Discussion for Insight – possible topics you may want to cover. Remember this depends entirely on your class discussion and you may not even cover the suggestions stated here but your conversation may lead to something else.

Overall Goal of IE: Make the learner more changeable, open to learning, and self-regulated. They become AWARE and more in charge of their own learning.

Instrumental Enrichment is not just about getting the correct answers. You are teaching **cognitive behaviors** or thinking skills as found in the Process Standards of the Common Core State Standards (CCSS). These cognitive behaviors are aligned to the following sources in the CCSS:

<u>English Language Arts</u>
Qualities of Students Who Are College and Career Ready in Writing, Speaking and Listening
<u>Mathematics</u>
Characteristics of Mathematically Proficient Students

The student must be an active participant in this process of change. It is your job to increase the student's awareness of his or her own thinking so that they experience a deeper understanding, not just you. The big idea is NOT to finish the sheet or find the correct answers, (though finishing the sheet with correct answers helps crystalize concepts). Rather, it is to cause the student to change his or her own thinking through mediation (MLE). You must be very intentional in your responses/questioning to increase this awareness and empower the student. Catch them being brilliant or notice when they are doing something desired. For example, "I noticed you didn't erase that one. You made a plan before beginning which showed a restraint of impulsivity."

Remember, the ultimate goal is to empower the student to develop the ability to mediate themselves.

IE Survival Guide
Organization of Dots

Organization of Dots introduces every thinking skill. Many of these thinking skills become their own instrument later on.

<u>Goals</u>
Duplicate a model according to a rule.
Use cues and strategies in the construction of a plan.

<u>Big Idea: Making order out of chaos</u>
- Perceive order
- Find order
- Develop a need for order

There is so much potential for mediation on each page of this instrument. What follows are only suggestions. It is important to allow the students' to do their work and to let your observations drive the mediation. For example, if you plan to talk about precision but the students change strategies, notice the change in strategy and make the students aware of that change in strategy. There will be plenty of opportunities to talk about precision on another page.

Cover Page

In my experience, I have realized that I don't need to endlessly repeat the individual pieces of the cover page. In other words, don't spend so much time on each part that you lose students' interest. The following are constructs and ideas for potential discussions. Don't do them all at once since you will have 13 more opportunities (one for each instrument) to cover the salient points.

Logo (a thinker) - simple, memorable, visual (you may have the student put their picture here).
Discuss "What does it mean to think?"

- Brainstorm: recalling, remembering, reflecting, making decisions, having ideas, solving problems, planning to do something, imagining, anticipating, and drawing conclusions.

Talk about problem solving. What is involved?

- Make a chart. Do this collectively with your students. Identify the problem, gather information (through our senses – give examples), consider possible courses of action/solutions, make a plan, carry out the plan, and check for accuracy.

Example: I use a hypothetical problem – I need to ride my bike but I can't. What's the problem? Is it the tire? The chain?

PAGE 20 in FIE teacher's manual helps in having students create a mind map that can be added to throughout this instrument.

Title - *Organization of Dots*
Talk about what it means to organize. Why do we organize? To create order, save time, be more efficient, to help understand the connection between things. Give examples of organization such as:

- food in a grocery store
- books in a library
- clothes in a dresser or closet
- items in a newspaper
- classrooms in a school
- time (minutes, hours, days, or weeks)

- class schedules
- TV schedules, bus or airplane schedules
- periods in history (eras and ages)
- money (family budget)
- government (federal, state, or local)

Symbol - Big Dipper - rotates around Polaris (the North Star). The **orientation** changes but the **relationship** does not.

Slogan - "Just a Moment . . . LET ME THINK!" This remains the same throughout all the Standard Instruments. It conveys an idea of calmness of the mind. We have time to think and thinking takes time. Some answers take more time to think through than others. It is normal/necessary to think before completing a task.

In *Mind Set* Carol Dweck says that people with fixed mind sets believe smart people already know and therefore don't need time to think. However, a person who has a growth mind set believes learning is a process which takes time and effort. This also helps with restraining impulsivity. Encourage students to think before they act/answer.

Page 1

Things to Consider
Introduce the "pencils down for discussion" rule. Dots can be so irresistible that many students will want to work during discussion. It's important that you make it clear to them that the discussion is more important than the task. Nobody makes a living connecting dots. Make it a challenge; "be strong enough to restrain your impulsivity." You may want to show the page before you give it to them (e.g. using a document reader) for pre-task discussion below.

At the beginning of each page say, "Scan the page. What do you notice?" If necessary, talk about what it means to scan.

Using **precise language** and **labeling** will be key vocabulary. Also introduce the terms **frame, column, row,** and **model**. Show them that this is a tool to talk about any part of the sheet precisely; "second row, third frame."

Rules of the Game (Organization of Dots)
There are rules to everything we do and there are reasons for each rule. What are the rules for crossing a street, dressing for school? What are the rules in a sport? You supply the rules to *Organization of Dots* and ask the students to think of possible reasons for each rule.

Rules to *Organization of Dots*
1. Use every dot once and only once
2. The figures must be identical in shape and size to those in the model
3. The shape and size of the figure stays the same even if there is a change in orientation (direction)
4. Work in order - left to right and top to bottom
5. Do not turn the page

Possible Reasons for These Rules
1. There are just enough dots in each frame to complete the figures in the model.
2. There are a lot of ways to connect the dots but only one way will give the desired result.

3. Changing orientation doesn't change an object. For example, a CD case is still a CD case whether it is standing upright on a shelf or lying flat on a table, right side up or upside down.

4. Turning the page might initially make the task easier, but we are learning to solve problems other than connecting dots. Again, nobody makes a living connecting dots. We cannot always manipulate the problem (rotate the page) to come up with a correct solution.

Work on the Sheet

Turn the students loose to work on the sheet. Tell them to complete the first two rows. Of course, your students will work at different rates. Give those who finish first permission to go on. Circulate, notice, and mediate. When you see that everyone has finished the first two rows, call the students back. Tell them to put their pencils down. Ask, "How were you able to find the figures?" Ask students to name strategies, write them on the board (or on chart paper) and label them with the name of the student that described it. Ask, "Who else used Sally's strategy?" This discussion is important for a variety of reasons. It makes kids aware of their own thinking and it gives them an opportunity to:
- articulate their thinking
- hear other strategies
- begin to see that there is not just one right way to do things

After the discussion, give students more time to complete the page, encouraging them to try other strategies if theirs is not working.

Closure - Discussion for Insight

It is imperative to have a short closing discussion at the end of each IE lesson. This has been a huge lesson, so limit the discussion to one important idea. Possibilities include: rules, planning behavior, strategies, precise language or restraining impulsivity.

Page 1A

Things to Consider
Order matters. Find the squares first. Otherwise, if you find the triangle first, you may have used half a square.

Work on the Sheet
Assign first two rows. Those that finish may work ahead. Encourage students to notice and use cues:
- larger dots in a frame
- colored dots in a frame
- Row 2, frames 1 and 2 contain dots in the same positions but there are no cues in frame 2

Call the students back. Tell them to put their pencils down. Ask, "How were you able to find the figures?" Ask students to name strategies, write them on the board (or on chart paper) and label these strategies with the name of the student that described it. Ask, "Who else used Sally's strategy?" This discussion is important for a variety of reasons. Kids become aware of their own thinking and the discussion gives them an opportunity to:
- articulate their thinking
- hear other strategies
- begin to see that there is not just one right way to do things

After the discussion, give students more time to complete the page. Encourage them to try other strategies if theirs is not working.

Closure - Discussion for Insight
Use this opportunity to take up some of the discussion you didn't have time for in the last lesson.

Possibilities include:
- Precise language/labeling – in talking about the page (rows, frames) and in talking about the figures (square, triangle, right angle)
- Planning and restraining impulsivity
- Having a strategy

- Checking back to a model
- Thinking about your own thinking

Page 1B

Things to Consider
The use of cues changes on this page. Color is used as a distractor. The blue dots do not define a singular shape as in previous pages, but **at times** one dot (sometimes blue, sometimes black) cues for each shape. This requires a switch in thinking and provides a great opportunity for discussing switching strategies when one strategy no longer works.

Work on the Sheet
Have students work on the first two rows. If some finish early, they can work ahead.

Call the students back. Tell them to put their pencils down. Ask students to name the strategies. Write them on the board (or on chart paper) and label each strategy with the name of the student that described it. Again, you can ask, "Who else used Sally's strategy?" This discussion is important for a variety of reasons. Kids become aware of their own thinking and the discussion gives them an opportunity to:
- articulate their thinking
- hear other strategies
- begin to see that there is not just one right way to do things

Give students more time to complete the page. Encourage them to try other strategies if theirs is not working.

Closure - Discussion for Insight
This discussion covers the same themes listed in previous pages (rules, planning behavior, strategies, precise language or restraining impulsivity) but includes new strategies.

Page E1 – Find the Error

Things to Consider
This page is about identifying errors and analyzing them. It is an opportunity to talk about error analysis in terms of input, elaboration, and output.

First define each term:
- **Input** -gathering information. For example, you got the wrong answer because you used the wrong numbers.
- **Elaboration** - using that information to perform the thinking. For example, you thought 6 X 7 was 48
- **Output** - expressing the answer. For example, you transposed the numbers and wrote 24 for 42.

Work on the Sheet
Have students work on the first two rows. If some finish early, they can work ahead.

Call the students back. Tell them to put their pencils down. Ask them to describe their strategies. In this discussion, you want to elicit from kids inferential thinking and have them use counting as a strategy to define the error – **L**arge Figure, **S**maller Figure, **M**issing Dot or **E**xtra Dot. For example, if there are too many dots the error is **E**xtra Dots. Not enough dots, the error is **M**issing Dots. The right number of dots is either **S**maller or **L**arger figure. However, in every frame of the first two rows (except for the first frame), only ONE of the squares will exactly reflect the model.

Closure - Discussion for Insight
By identifying the error, we can correct it and possibly prevent it from happening again.

Mind Set by Carol Dweck - while we don't seek to make them, errors do not make us bad, they are opportunities for learning.

Page 2

Things to Consider
Dots are getting closer together. Thus the task becomes more complex.

Color is sometimes used as a cue (one dot for each figure) but not always.

Work on the Sheet
Ask students, "What do you notice?" Dots are closer together (increasing complexity). This requires the use of strategies in problem solving. Some of these include:
- Systematic search
- Process of elimination - making order out of chaos
- Visual cues
- Restraining impulsivity
- Recognizing relationships
- Finding the square first (inferential thinking)

Students need to develop a strategy in the absence of cues. Strategies switch to applying attributes of squares and right triangles. Talk about the language of attributes:
- parallel
- perpendicular
- right angle
- length
- number of corners
- number of sides

Closure - Discussion for Insight
Have students think about what was the same on this page compared to the first few? What was different? Which frame was the most difficult for you (various answers)? Anticipate row 2, frame 1. This one is a real challenge due to the two extremely close dots which are a part of each triangle's acute angle.

Page E2

Things to Consider
This error page introduces one new figure as a possible error – a rectangle.

Color may be used as a distractor (see row two, frame two).

Work on the Sheet
Depending on your class, you may or may not have students work through the whole sheet.

Closure - Discussion for Insight
The same mistake can be caused for different reasons. Knowing the source of an error can help to prevent its occurrence. Identifying an error can enable us to fix it.

Implicit directions: even though we are not told to write a letter on the line and draw an arrow to the spot the error occurs, we know to do it because the model shows it. Sometimes we know to do something even though we are not explicitly told.

Using a code: we know what "S", "L", and "R" mean, but a stranger in our classroom might not know the code. Everybody in our class agreed to use the code and understood it. For others not present when the agreement was made, a key to the code is necessary.

Things to Consider
More complex figures require labeling of unfamiliar, non-standard shapes

Systematic search and problem solving strategies

Use points of reference and switch strategies when the cues fade

Work on the Sheet
Introduce the idea of universal labels vs agreed upon labels. If we agree to call the figure an hourglass, it gives us language to talk about the figure so that everyone understands what we are talking about. Have the students give the figures specific names.

Closure - Discussion for Insight
Are students erasing less? Point it out. This is restraint of impulsivity.

Complex vs difficult - It is possible that the students had an easier time doing the work on this sheet than they did on the first sheet. Ask them why. Their responses may include practice and specific strategies. Just because something is complex, it doesn't make it difficult. This is an important idea that mediates competency in students. When they are faced with a challenging situation, they can remember complexity does not make something impossible. They can recall strategies to deal with complexity: scaffolding, finding a starting point, breaking the task into smaller pieces. Also, the more practice you have with a task the easier it becomes.

Having labels for things that are concrete or abstract helps us make sense of those things in our minds so that we can understand and use that information. For example, signs help us get places. Labels on items in the grocery store tell us how many calories are in each item. Labels help us solve problems. Labels make our lives easier to manage.

Page E3

Things to Consider
Repeated practice with using a key, identifying errors and restraining impulsivity

Good practice for overcoming blocking

Work on the Sheet
Incorrect Form – this error is introduced for the first time

Closure - Discussion for Insight
Keys are often used to abbreviate larger ideas. Examples include abbreviations such as NBA (National Basketball Association) or the compass rose on a map.

Discuss errors - the errors on these pages are not the focus – we a need to make the connection to mistakes made in life.
- Everybody makes mistakes
- You don't need to quit or start completely over if you can identify and correct the part that has an error
- Some mistakes matter more than others

Page 4

Things to Consider
Added complexity: asymmetrical figures. Talk about the meaning of symmetrical and asymmetrical.

The necessity for deferred decision making can be discussed on this page.

Work on the Sheet
After students have worked on rows one and two, ask them what they notice about row three before they begin the task. The dots are much closer together and cues diminish from given lines to colored dots.

The cues use the strategy of finding the "L" from the hexagon, but students may switch to finding the rectangle first (the parallel lines and close proximity of end dots make it easier to find). Four possible dots are eliminated when this is done.

Deferred decision making - In several frames there appear to be two choices for the large "L" that forms part of the concave hexagon (row 5 frame 4 has two possibilities for rectangles).

Closure - Discussion for Insight
Many times it is necessary to put off making a decision so you can look at all the possibilities, e.g. buying a house or a car. These are big decisions. People want to feel good about their choices.

What can happen when decisions are made without all of the available information? For example, they can decide against reading a book before they have read anything about it or they might decide to get angry before hearing all sides of a story.

Page 5

Things to Consider
This page introduces a *curvilinear* figure and how we might cope or deal with something unfamiliar.

Work on the Sheet
Establish names for the figures; mitten and sled have been used by some of my classes. It doesn't matter what the students agree upon, just that they have a common language so that everyone understands what is being said.

Strategies to help find curvilinear figures:
- A counting strategy is helpful for the mitten; six dots form the curved line of the mitten, acute and obtuse angles for the "thumb" of the mitten.
- An equal distance idea for the sled – as if curved lines (arcs) could be parallel, also the side lines are parallel.
- Check back to the model.
- Imagine how things will look if they are turned in different orientations.

Closure - Discussion for Insight
Difficult vs complex. For example, driving a car is more complex than running.

There are many ways of coping with change - situations that are new or different. For example, if you move or have a new baby in the house you will need to acquire different strategies to handle that change.

Page 6

Things to Consider
The more entangled the task, the more difficult the frame.

This page uses both universal and non-universal labels. It reinforces the necessity for flexibility and yet unchanging strategies to find the figures.

The student must be aware of the need for precision.

Work on the Sheet
Establish labels: star and curved figure (boot).

Intrinsic cues (built into the figure): big dots, colored dots, line segments, and the rule of the figure.

Extrinsic cues - cues that are not part of the figure itself but lead us to it.

It is possible to find the star by finding the square formed by the four dots toward the center. Lines are not drawn between these dots, but the dots are used to find the remaining four dots which form the points of the star.

Use the counting strategy from page five to find the curvilinear line of the curved figure.

Where to start? Find the star first; it's easier because it is symmetrical. The remaining dots will form the curved figure (using logic).

Precision is important: close dots make the following frames difficult – row 3 frames 2, 3, and 4; row 4 frames 2, 3, and 4.

Closure - Discussion for Insight
Where do we see cues in life? Give directions using the address, color, size of a house (intrinsic). Or give directions using reference

points, turn by the Target store across the street from a playground (extrinsic).

When is it necessary to be precise? Possibilities include: spelling words, administering medication or in a photo finish race.

Page 7

Things to Consider
Introduction of *collinear* lines

Precision in labeling cues

Work on the Sheet
Identify and name the figures:
- Right-angled U: extrinsic cue – I can see two rectangles, one made of the outer 4 dots and the other made of the inner 4 dots.
- Diamond: intrinsic cues – 2 acute and 2 obtuse angles. They are equal length sides.
- Kite – extrinsic cue – there are three dots that form a triangle, intrinsic cue – acute angle, length of sides.

When choosing which shape to find first, use a hierarchy of cues from easiest to more difficult. Start with U shape because right angles are the easiest to work with. This eliminates the most dots.

Closure - Discussion for Insight
Many times we must establish our own cues in a new situation or task. For example, when we find our way around without street signs or when we are able to fix something without the manual. This creates a feeling of competency. Make students aware of the relative ease with which they did the page. This is so much more complex than what they started with.

Page 8

Things to Consider
Practice precision in labeling

Master a complex task by breaking it down into smaller pieces

Make a detailed plan

Work on the Sheet
Name the figures. Possibilities include right angle G and L, then observe attributes of each. You may want to introduce the word "orthogonal," meaning consisting of, or involving right angles.

Your starting point, use logic. If I find the G first, I use ten dots and only have six left for the L.

A possible new strategy? Find the four collinear dots then connect the first and second and the third and fourth but not the second and third.

Closure - Discussion for Insight
Contrast the relative ease of dealing with the familiar with the difficulty of dealing with the unfamiliar. Is it easier if you have precise labels? Is it easier if you break it down into smaller pieces and have a plan before you start? For example, when you write a story or work on a complex math problem, you need to break down the steps that make the story work and the steps that solve the math problem. You need precision in your words to communicate your thoughts. Precision must exist to get the right thoughts. In any math problem, precision must exist to get the right answer.

Page 9

Things to Consider
Focus on parts of the whole. Notice that the shapes do not always contain right angles.

Optical illusion – things are not always as they seem.

Work on the Sheet
Label the figures: pants, rectangle, parallelogram (universal and non-universal labels).

Length of side will not help you because the lengths are too much the same: the bottom of the pant leg and the side of the parallelogram are the same length, the short side of the rectangle is close to the same. The top of the pants and the longer side of the parallelogram are the same length. The long sides of the rectangle and the long pants are the same length.

Build your own strategy: perhaps the extrinsic cue of the triangle in the pants, intrinsic cue of right angles of the rectangle, and parallel lines of parallelogram and rectangle.

Closure - Discussion for Insight
Notice the parts of a whole. If you break the writing of poetry into parts and phrases, it makes the writing easier.

Sometimes things are not as they first appear. For example, at first, you may think someone is an angry person, but when you get to know them you realize they aren't who you thought they were.

Page 10

Things to Consider
This page is a review of the strategies covered so far but the task is more complex: a figure within a figure, regular and irregular hexagons.

Changing or adding a rule: using one dot to connect three line segments.

Work on the Sheet
Notice how close the dots are clustered in the last few frames.

Have students notice details. Notice that the lines forming the top and bottom of the regular hexagon which are parallel to the lines at the top and bottom of the house will narrow the choices of where to look for the roof to two choices.

Closure - Discussion for Insight
Many times, the first step in learning something new is to practice and review what we already know. For example, before writing a paper on mammals you need to review what you already know about them.

Page 11 (fish page)

Things to Consider
Greater complexity in the task is presented on this page. This task requires a more complex strategy. You also need to be very rigid in adherence to the rules.

Without disequilibrium, there is no need to stop, notice, and ask questions.

Deficiency – inappropriate lack of disequilibrium.

Work on the Sheet
Agree to labels: perhaps fat fish, skinny fish, and ship.

It will be helpful to take time at the beginning of the task to clearly define the problem. Also, take time to compare the two fish figures: same number of dots (seven), three dots form the body and head, and four dots form the tail for both. Notice the position of the eye relative to the dot. Notice the tail shape of each fish. Notice the ship - right angles and parallel lines are helpful. Extremely close dots of fat fish can be helpful.
Determine a starting place. Possibilities are as follows:
- Pick one eye and assume it is part of the skinny fish. Check the hypothesis. Draw the fish. The other eye belongs to the opposite fish. Find the ship last by finding the right angles in the remaining dots.
- Look for extremely close dots of fat fish's tail. Identify the rest of the tail and then complete the rest of the fish. The other eye belongs to skinny fish and the last six dots are the ship.
- Find the ship first using right angles and parallel lines. This eliminates six dots that might otherwise confuse the finding of the fish.

Closure - Discussion for Insight
Greater complexity - for example, when we build our robot for the LEGO FIRST League or solve a truancy problem in our school, we need a more complex strategy to solve the problem.

Many times in life we need to adhere strictly to the rules. For example, when filling out a college application, you need to answer every question and attach all supporting documentation or they will not even consider your application.

Ask the students, "What have you learned about yourself as a learner?"

Page 12 (3-D page)

Things to Consider
Introduce three dimensional figures – increased complexity.

Notice the "three line segments meeting at one dot rule" from page 10 is in effect for this page, i.e. one dot helps you connect three lines (but remember each dot is only used once).

Work on the Sheet
One strategy is to use the given cues. However, when cues are absent, you need a new strategy. For example, find the flat polygons, and then add the 3-D part.

Closure - Discussion for Insight
You never found figures like this before. What enabled you to accomplish the goal? Possibilities include:

- When presented with a new, complex task, we connect the task to what we are already familiar with and build from there.
- Take time before you start. Get a clear picture of what is needed.

Discussion of last frame – it looks like a big jumble of dots. To accomplish the goal, students stayed calm, looked systematically, used a strategy and reminded themselves they could do it.

Connection to real life – adding dimension allows us to connect and understand things more realistically because the more properties (color, sight [dimension], sound, or smell) we can attach to new learning, the greater chance it will stick. For example, when we read a book and then see the movie or act out the story, we are more likely to have a greater understanding and remember the salient points.

Page 13

Things to Consider
Repeated practice with three dimensional figures.

Work on the Sheet
Affirmation - look how far we have come! You can accomplish difficult and complex tasks if you remain calm, gather relevant information, find an appropriate strategy, work systematically with precision, and believe in yourself.

Closure - Discussion for Insight
Summarize the instrument. Ask students what they learned in the instrument. Have them make a web or mind map which will be displayed in the room for future reference.

IE Survival Guide
Orientation in Space I

<u>Goal</u>
Orientation in Space I is about spatial orientation, its representation and communication

<u>Big Ideas</u>
- Simple system - left, right, front and back
- Spatial relationships
- Reduction of egocentrism/point of view

There is so much potential for mediation on each page of this instrument. What follows are only suggestions. It is important to allow the students' to do their work and to let your observations drive the mediation. For example, if you plan to talk about precision but the students change strategies, notice the change in strategy and make the students aware of that change in strategy. There will be plenty of opportunities to talk about precision on another page.

Cover Page

In my experience, I have realized that I don't need to endlessly repeat the individual pieces of the cover page. In other words, don't spend so much time on each part that you lose students' interest. The following are constructs and ideas for potential discussions. Don't do them all at once since you will have 12 more opportunities (one for each instrument) to cover the salient points.

Logo (a thinker) - simple, memorable, visual (you may have the student put their picture here).
Discuss "What does it mean to think?"

- Brainstorm: recalling, remembering, reflecting, making decisions, having ideas, solving problems, planning to do something, imagining, anticipating, and drawing conclusions.

Talk about problem solving. What is involved?

- Make a chart. Do this collectively with your students. Identify the problem, gather information (through our senses – give examples), consider possible courses of action/solutions, make a plan, carry out the plan, and check for accuracy.

Example: I use a hypothetical problem – I need to ride my bike but I can't. What's the problem? Is it the tire? The chain?

Title – *Orientation in Space I.*

Symbol – Elicit a comparison of the symbol to paths or street intersections. Notice the arrows, universal signs for indicating direction. Discuss possible routes, ways of getting from point to point on the symbol, shortcuts.

Ask, "What does *orientation* mean? (*Familiarity with* as in orientation day at school as opposed to *disoriented* feeling when you first wake up in a strange place).

Ask, "What is space?" (Distance in all directions – two as on the paper or three-dimensional in most of life. Personal space is a comfortable distance between people).

Both orientation and space can be used with abstract concepts such as "crossroads" in our lives; decisions that we make.

Slogan - "Just a Moment . . . LET ME THINK!" This remains the same throughout all the Standard Instruments. It conveys an idea of calmness of the mind. We have time to think and thinking takes time. Some answers take more time to think through than others. It is normal/necessary to think before completing a task.

In *Mind Set* Carol Dweck says that people with fixed mind sets believe smart people already know and therefore don't need time to think. However, a person who has a growth mind set believes learning is a process which takes time and effort. This also helps with restraining impulsivity. Encourage students to think before they act/answer.

Page 1

Things to Consider
This is about creating the need to analyze a symbol and relate the object to the perceiver.

Introduction of the *concept* of orientation in space (a closed system: front, back, left and right).

We use many words for front, back, left and right (trees, flowers, house, etc.). Sometimes these words are spatial and sometimes they are figural.

Words have a values slant.

Work on the Sheet
Ask students to scan the page and then ask "What do you notice?"

This page introduces a closed system: front, back, left, right. To know one member, is to know them all.
What are some other closed systems?
- Days of the week (if you know Sunday then you know the next day is Monday, the day before was Saturday…)
- Counting numbers
- The alphabet
- Seasons of the year, months of the year

Discussion questions:
While facing the class, ask students to raise their right hand (you raise yours). Why do we have opposite hands up? If I turn to the side, where is my front? Back? Left? Right? Through discussion students will realize that the relative position between front, back, left and right do not change when orientation (direction of front) changes.

Does everything have a front, back, left, and right side? Students might initially say yes. Let them share ideas. What about a tree, a table, a dinner plate? These things might have a front and back, left and right but this is only relative to the person viewing it.

Ask: What does it mean when I say, "Stand in front of the tree so I can take your picture?"

Closure - Discussion for Insight
The concept of space is used in almost all of our experiences and tasks. For example, we have space between:
- Each other at the lunch table
- Ourselves and the computer screen
- Words on a page

Page 2

Things to Consider
A change in the orientation of the system (front, back, left, right - where the boy carries the system) results in a change in the relationship.

Use of precise language: "The tree is to the (right, left, front, back) of the boy.

Work on the Sheet
Scan the page. There are no written instructions. What are we to do? (Infer what is expected by gathering relevant cues and prior experience).
Only the boy moves, the other elements are stable. A change in the boy's orientation changes what he sees and changes his relationship to the objects.

Closure - Discussion for Insight
Our perception of objects or events is perceived according to **our** point of view. The same object or event may look different to different people. A person standing in the same spot but facing a different direction will have a different perception. The same event can be perceived differently by different people. For example:
- a child gets a day off from school on a snow day but a snow plow operator works a 12 hour shift
- a rainy day ruins a family picnic but a gardener rejoices for a rain on his parched plants
- a twenty dollar bill is precious to a homeless person but is chump change to a millionaire

Things to Consider
Everyone has a personal system of reference.

Develop representational thinking, the ability to visually transport an object, and represent information in a table.

In each table there are three variables which are dependent on one another. We have two pieces of given information and one piece is missing. We see this in math, e.g. $3 + 2 = ?$, $3 + ? = 5$ or $? + 2 = 5$. Can we deduce the answer? Yes!

Work on the Sheet
Practice using precise language: "When the boy is in position (A, B, C, or D) the object is to the (front, back, left, or right)."

Talk about how charts and tables are useful tools to convey information. Elicit examples from the students.

Closure - Discussion for Insight
Oftentimes we must *choose* our orientation or position toward things. For example, position A might be the easiest to work with. Why? (It is easier to work with a position that is like ours. It is more difficult to work with a position different from ours). This is true for collaborative work as well as physically. Other examples, in math, we must choose which operation to do first and in relationships we must choose who to talk to first to help us solve a problem.

Page 4

Things to Consider
Develop representational thinking.

Use several sources of information to arrive at a conclusion.

Work on the Sheet
Many things can be learned from charts. We already use them in school to gather and relate information. For example, the daily schedule, a times table chart or sports scores.

Have students use precise language. Ask, "When the object is to the (left, right, front, or back) of the boy he is in position (A, B, C ,or D)?"

Closure – Discussion for Insight
Look at examples of charts (school calendar or other) to determine what kind of information can be gleaned from a chart?

Representational thinking: the ability to perceive something with no sensory support, especially important in cases where trial and error will not work. For example, how will the room look after it is painted? How will the kitchen look after a homeowner installs a granite countertop? People cannot make an informed decision if they don't like how it looks. How will my hair look after it is cut? How will letters written in permanent marker look on a poster?

Page 5

Things to Consider

Develop representational thinking and flexibility in switching between the part asked for - object, position, and side of the person.

Use several sources of information.

Gather information from a table.

Work on the Sheet

Lines 9, 10, and 14 are interesting for discussion: they have 8 possible answers (4 positions and 4 sides).

Closure - Discussion for Insight

When there are no pre-set conditions or absolutes, our options are wide open. For example, if someone gave you $10 and told you to spend it anyway you wanted to, you can spend it any way you choose. When you have a free day off from school, you can do as you please.

When there are absolutes in orientation, and mistakes are made, what is the nature of the mistake? Front/back mistakes are rarely made. Left/right mistakes are more common. Why?

Things to Consider
Clear communication of relevant information.

Students should be able to discriminate between the concepts of side and direction.

Work on the Sheet
- Have students label the people – man, woman, boy with hat, boy without hat.
- Discuss the relationship of one to the other with each serving as the referent. How does the sentence change when shifting from point of view of one to point of view of another?
- If each person turns the way they appear to be turning, are they facing each other? Which people will be going the same direction?
- Encourage students to describe other scenarios about where the people are going.

Closure - Discussion for Insight
Direction matters when:
- We are giving directions and the (direction we are coming from) makes a difference.
- We are referring to position. It doesn't just refer to physical position. In order to understand other viewpoints we must be able to assume the position of the other person. Understanding another viewpoint doesn't mean we have to agree with it. There are times when our own viewpoint can also change.

In school, directions may matter when looking for specific information out of a book. You may need to look in the index or table of contents. Also, directions matter when you need to put something together in a specific order (like a swing set).

Page 7

Things to Consider
Contrast information presented in pictures and with symbols. Note a higher degree of abstraction than on page two.

Review the system, communicate clearly, and introduce the use of symbols to represent reality.

Work on the Sheet
Discussion of traces, symbols, and signs - traces are evidence of presence. For example:

- **Traces** are evidence of presence of a human's fingerprints, feces or footprints of an animal. Traces are the most proximal to the real thing.
- **Symbols** represent an object or idea. For example, the male and female icons on a bathroom door are more abstract but carry an association to the real object.
- **Signs** are the most abstract, for example arithmetic signs.

Closure - Discussion for Insight
Signs and symbols are used to represent things in real life. Where do we use/see traces, symbols, and signs? Let the students come up with examples: traces – lipstick on a glass, food residue on a plate, fingerprints, footprints, and other evidence that something was there. Traces can be signs or symbols. For example, the heart symbol meaning love (I [heart] dogs)

Page 8

Things to Consider
The task is to identify the position of the dot in relationship to the arrow. This task is more abstract but the task is the same as on page three.

On the top half of the page, given the arrow and the dot, name which side the dot is on. On page three, students were given the boy and the object, and then asked which side of the boy the object was located.

On the bottom half of the pages, given the arrow and the position, draw the dot. On page three, given the position (direction boy was facing) and the side of the boy, name the object.

Work on the Sheet
Have students complete the page.

Closure - Discussion for Insight
It is important to know where we stand in relation to other things. In school, you must know where you stand in relation to your grades or in relation to a friend.

What is the range of possibility when placing a dot to the right of the arrow? To the left? Front? Back? Does distance matter? The white board is in front of you whether you sit in the front or in the back of the room.

Clear communication: "The dot is….."

Page 9

Things to Consider
The verbal code must be translated into an action.

Work on the Sheet
Compare this page to page four where the side of person and object are given and the position must be deciphered. Here, object (dot) and side are given.

There are many possible correct solutions to these examples. Some answers, while technically correct, may not fulfill the spirit of the task. For example, row three, frames one or two: squeezing an arrow in between the dot and the frame border.

Closure - Discussion for Insight
When concepts become more abstract, to help make sense of the situation, we need to connect them to things/people (relationships) we are already familiar with. For example, a teacher may want to introduce multiplication through repeated addition.

We need to be open to more than one correct answer or more than one way to do something. How to make choices when there is more than one correct answer? Examples include: paying 52 cents: should you use 2 quarters and 2 pennies? 5 dimes and 2 pennies? 1 quarter, 2 dimes, a nickel, and 2 pennies? 52 pennies?

In what instances are technically "correct" solutions not acceptable? For example, paying $5 with 500 pennies while technically correct is not the most efficient.

Page 10

Things to Consider
This is a summary of *Orientation in Space I*.

Reinforcement of flexibility by changing tasks from frame to frame.

Provides practice in identifying and constructing relationships.

Work on the Sheet
More abstract than previous pages and there are infinite possibilities for some frames.

Closure - Discussion for Insight
Can we put ourselves in someone else's shoes? For example, if someone doesn't speak English, can we understand how difficult their understanding of a task may be? When someone gets hurt, can we understand how they feel?

IE Survival Guide
Comparisons

<u>Goal</u>
Comparisons is about developing and recognizing parameters and relationships of comparative behavior.

<u>Big Ideas:</u>
- Develop a habit of noticing and comparing
- We compare according to attributes, qualities, properties, features
- Comparing is part of an important hierarchy of learning. When we first learn words and labeling, we need the ability to describe before we can compare. We must be able to compare in order to classify, to put things in systems to build a hierarchy, to lead to formal logical thinking (i.e. develop clear communication finding/using "just right sized" words).

There is so much potential for mediation on each page of this instrument. What follows are only suggestions. It is important to allow the students' to do their work and to let your observations drive the mediation. For example, if you plan to talk about precision but the students change strategies, notice the change in strategy and make the students aware of that change in strategy. There will be plenty of opportunities to talk about precision on another page.

Cover Page

In my experience, I have realized that I don't need to endlessly repeat the individual pieces of the cover page. In other words, don't spend so much time on each part that you lose students' interest. The following are constructs and ideas for potential discussions. Don't do them all at once since you will have 11 more opportunities (one for each instrument) to cover the salient points.

Logo (a thinker) - simple, memorable, visual (you may have the student put their picture here).
Discuss "What does it mean to think?"
- Brainstorm: recalling, remembering, reflecting, making decisions, having ideas, solving problems, planning to do something, imagining, anticipating, and drawing conclusions.

Talk about problem solving. What is involved?
- Make a chart: get students to list: identify the problem, gather information – (through our senses – give examples) consider possible courses of action/solutions, make a plan, carry out the plan, and check for accuracy.

Example: I use a hypothetical problem. I need to ride my bike but I can't. What's the problem? Is it the tire? The chain?

Title and Symbol - *Comparisons*
Ask the students what they notice. Discuss ways the circles are the same and different. There may be similarities in things that are different. There may be things that are different in things that are similar.
Discuss: Why do we compare? Give examples from your life when you compare.

All of our decisions and judgments are based on comparison.

Slogan - "Just a Moment . . . LET ME THINK!" This remains the same throughout all the Standard Instruments. It conveys an idea of calmness of the mind. We have time to think and thinking takes time. Some answers take more time to think through than others. It is normal/necessary to think before completing a task.

In *Mind Set* Carol Dweck says that people with fixed mind sets believe smart people already know and therefore don't need time to think. However, a person who has a growth mind set believes learning is a process which takes time and effort. This also helps with restraining impulsivity. Encourage students to think before they act/answer.

Page 1

Things to Consider
Describe commonalities and differences between people and objects

Work on the Sheet
Say, "Scan the page. What do you notice?"
Main idea: What are the attributes of comparison? Even though two objects may have obvious differences they may also have some attributes in common. What is important is the following:

- It is true
- It uses the right sized word
- It reflects knowledge/experience
- It is salient
- It stays with the same attribute (can't mix attributes)
- There is a reason or goal

Use right sized words. For the first picture, words that could be used for "common": boys (too big word), smiling (too small word), hair (too small), dimple (too small) or head (just right).

Closure - Discussion for Insight
Here is where we can also introduce "arguing" in the true sense of an argument, not a fight. We present our ideas with evidence to convince others to see our point of view. It is ok to disagree. If someone gives a compelling argument, you should agree, not stubbornly refuse just to be *right*. The answers on the page are not as important as students providing good evidence for their answers.

Page 2

Things to Consider
Comparison based on attributes

In order for this page:
shape direction/orientation, number, clarity/completeness (quality) or orientation.

Work on the Sheet
Again, say, "Scan the page. What do you notice?"
Have students compare attributes as described above:
Row 1: Shape
Row 2: Direction/orientation
Row 3: Number
Row 4: Clarity/completeness (quality)
Row 5: Orientation

Closure - Discussion for Insight
We compare for a purpose using a set of criteria. For example, we compare cars to see which is more economical on gas or we compare grocery stores to find out which one has the cheaper deal.

Page 3

Things to Consider
Comparing in a verbal modality

Words have a symbolic function

Work on the Sheet
When looking at a word, we can't see similarities or differences except in the length of a word, similar letters etc. Written words are symbols that represent ideas. We think about the meaning of the word and form ideas in our mind related to the word.

The power of this page is in the arguments students use to convince each other. Don't force the students to change their answers, but encourage them to listen. If they are swayed by an argument, they are welcome to change their answer. Notice the first student that does this and bring it to the attention of the class. Don't encourage students to be easily led to change their answers, but emphasize that we shouldn't stubbornly hold on to an idea when a better argument comes to light.

Closure - Discussion for Insight
It is easier to understand pictures and concrete things than words and abstract ideas. We know this because the brain more easily recognizes pictures than words. Not until at least the age of eight do we begin to think in words. For example, it is easier to read the picture on a road sign than the words on a sign.

Page 4

Things to Consider
This page covers the same concepts as page 3.

Work on the Sheet
This might be a good time to show students how to qualify statements with "generally speaking..." because exceptions can be found in many examples.

Closure - Discussion for Insight
In the discussion, you can talk about comparisons based on power, function, role, use and physical attributes as found in the teachers manual.

Pages 5 and 6 (taught together)

Things to Consider
Finding a superordinate concept or label for the way things are the same or different – temporal and spatial relationships. For example, one house is big, another is small. The superordinate concept is size. Heavy and light - the superordinate concept is weight.

Work on the Sheet
Have students work on the sheets naming the commonalities and differences. Then return to earlier pages, like page 1, and name the superordinate concepts.

Closure - Discussion for Insight
Choosing requires comparing. For example, choosing a topic to write about or choosing your favorite restaurant requires comparison to what you already know or have experienced.

Page 7

Things to Consider
This page is about finding identical things (sharing ALL attributes) in two of five pictures. Students need to develop a strategy for searching for identical things.
Definition of identical – exactly the same in all ways or sharing ALL attributes.

Work on the Sheet
Compare five pictures to find the two that are identical. Have students describe their strategies - the first ones are less complex. Scanning might be a strategy. As the figures get more complex (rows six and seven), closer attention to detail is required. Systematic search and process of elimination are strategies to discuss.

Closure - Discussion for Insight
Where is close attention to detail in comparison necessary in life? Phone numbers that differ by only one or two digits, addresses, your car in a parking lot – there may be other cars of your make and model.

Past events, experiences, relationships create expectations. Do acquaintances of older siblings expect you to be similar in your behavior? Is the McDonald's hamburger you just ate just like the one you had last week?

Page 8

Things to Consider
Ranking objects according to their similarities or differences to a model.

This page seems simple at first. Students will think they have <u>the</u> right answer.

Work on the Sheet
Discuss row 1. Is the order 3 1 2 5 4 or 4 5 1 3 2 correct? These rankings are based on number of points or position of points.
- Ranking is relative and is a judgment call
- You can only rank according to one attribute at a time
- Whoever controls the attributes controls the comparison and therefore the ranking

Closure - Discussion for Insight
Some things may be very close to the model, a goal or an idea, but they cannot substitute for the real thing.

Ask students what kinds of things they rank. For example, rank soft drinks or relationships (best friend). Prioritizing requires ranking. When we make a choice we rank something over another.

Page 9

Things to Consider
Students must compare to a given model. There may be similarities and there may be confusion in that process but this is a wonderful opportunity for mediation.

Form = outside shape

Work on the Sheet
It may be helpful to have the students label the second column, "A", and the third column, "B." This will make it easier to discuss the examples.
Expect disequilibrium on this page. We are not trying to prevent it. Definition of form – outside shape, formation may be the word for what occurs on the fourth row.

Closure - Discussion for Insight
Whoever controls the attributes controls the comparison. This is seen in advertising and politics. For example, Cadillac ignores price in favor of comfort and luxury but Honda ignores luxury, in favor of price and gas mileage.

What things can be similar and still be ok to use? For example, baseball bats or tennis racquets are not all the same (different brands, etc.) but they are all regulation size.

Page 10

Things to Consider
On this page you have to use systematic search to increase precision.

Students have to be able to consider several sources of information, compare two things, and stick to a definition.

Work on the Sheet
Have students locate and describe five differences between two pictures.
Ask students to explain their strategies, such as systematic search, attention to detail.

Closure - Discussion for Insight
When making a comparison, it is often necessary to be very precise. For example, when you conduct a science experiment or read the fine print on a contract, you need to be very precise.

Page 11

Things to Consider
This page is similar to page nine - comparing to a given model. However, instead of finding what is common you have to find the differences.

Work on the Sheet
Work on this page in the same manner as on page nine.

Closure - Discussion for Insight
There are times when differences are important even though similarities exist, e.g. finding your car in a parking lot at a football game.

Page 12

Things to Consider
Spend a lot of time here on planning behavior and restraint of impulsivity. The head is the planner; the pencil is the recorder.

Talk about stable and relative attributes.

Work on the Sheet
Model the first row on the board.

Closure - Discussion for Insight
Consider more than one piece of information at a time.

What are examples of things/places that have shared attributes, e.g. schools, shoes, or math.

Page 13

Things to Consider
Similar to page 12, however, you have to make a drawing that is different from the sample.

Work on the Sheet
Students will notice that preserving one attribute while changing another is not always easy.

Closure - Discussion for Insight
Many things and situations in life have shared attributes even though they may seem very different. For example, in poetry, you may keep the same form but change the topic.

Page 14

Things to Consider
Describe similarities and differences.

This page is an introduction to set theory. Use common attributes to place members in a set. Discriminate between members and nonmembers of a set.

Work on the Sheet
The first column contains members of the set

The second column is the set name

The third column names the attributes being considered

Closure - Discussion for Insight
Comparison is a lead into classification. This is why vocabulary is critical in any subject. Think of a subject:
- English (set name)
    - ✓ Member may be literature, short stories, poetry, etc.
- Mathematics classes (set name)
    - ✓ Members may include geometry, algebra or calculus.

Pages 15 and 16 (taught together)

Things to Consider
Demonstrates mastery of the instrument and again asks you to describe similarities and differences.

Work on the Sheet
Select items that fit a set and a subset. They are similar according to one attribute and different according to another attribute. Under column two (Common) have the students write "Set Name."

Closure - Discussion for Insight
Many times we use one word that describes the set name. However, what we are talking about may be very complex. For example, cook, marketing, or listen can mean different things. It requires you to be more precise in the context and may require a greater definition of attributes. There may be many steps in the process.

IE Survival Guide
Analytic Perception

Goal
Analytic Perception is about <u>differentiation</u> (taking apart) and <u>integration</u> (putting together).

Big Ideas:
Perception is not being encountered here for the first time but needs its own instrument for emphasis. For example, in reviewing the other instruments, perception is there as follows:
Organization of Dots – students must seek a small part in a larger, more complex whole
Orientation in Space – students must see left, right, front, and back as parts of a system, each standing in relationship to the other components.
Comparisons – students have to decide among all possible attributes of an item which are the most salient attributes for the particular comparison.

- What are the origins of things? Nothing exists complete. Every single person or thing is/has a part(s) and at the same time is part of a greater whole. For example, we eat bread which comes from a wheat field and at the same time each piece of bread is a whole unto itself.
- When we are able to identify and label both the whole and individual parts, we are able to better understand relationships (concrete and affective) and use them to organize information and solve problems.

There is so much potential for mediation on each page of this instrument. What follows are only suggestions. It is important to allow the students' to do their work and to let your observations drive the mediation. For example, if you plan to talk about precision but the students change strategies, notice the change in strategy and make the students aware of that change in strategy.

There will be plenty of opportunities to talk about precision on another page.

Cover Page

In my experience, I have realized that I don't need to endlessly repeat the individual pieces of the cover page. In other words don't spend so much time on each part that you lose students' interest. The following are constructs and ideas for potential discussions. Don't do them all at once since you will have 10 more opportunities (one for each instrument) to cover the salient points.

Logo (a thinker) - simple, memorable, visual (you may have the student put their picture here).
Discuss "What does it mean to think?"
- Brainstorm: recalling, remembering, reflecting, making decisions, having ideas, solving problems, planning to do something, imagining, anticipating, and drawing conclusions.

Talk about problem solving. What is involved?
- Make a chart. Do this collectively with your students. Identify the problem, gather information (through our senses – give examples), consider possible courses of action/solutions, make a plan, carry out the plan, and check for accuracy.

Example: I use a hypothetical problem – I need to ride my bike but I can't. What's the problem? Is it the tire? The chain?

Title – *Analytic Perception*

Symbol - Ask the students what they notice. Invite them to hypothesize the meaning of the symbol (our desire for closure, for gestalt, for wholeness) as we want to push the parts of the oval into their proper places. Don't be afraid to get a bit philosophical in these discussions. Why DO we want things to fit correctly and to complete unfinished things? Is that part of being a thinking human being? Explore the word **perception** and think with the students about how critical one's perception is in all situations. Explore the importance of others' perceptions to see the differences in things that are similar.

Slogan - "Just a Moment . . . LET ME THINK!" This remains the same throughout all the Standard Instruments. It conveys an idea of calmness of the mind. We have time to think and thinking takes time. Some answers take more time to think through than others. It is normal/necessary to think before completing a task.

In *Mind Set* Carol Dweck says that people with fixed mind sets believe smart people already know and therefore don't need time to think. However, a person who has a growth mind set believes learning is a process which takes time and effort. This also helps with restraining impulsivity. Encourage students to think before they act/answer.

Page 1

Things to Consider
Every whole can be divided into parts, and those parts can be differentiated by color, number, code or name.

Work on the Sheet
Have students get their colored pencils to do this page. Ask them, "How, in our world are wholes are divided into parts?" Have them come up with answers . . . by **color** (sections of a stadium, doors in a school, lines in the hallway of hospitals, lines in zoos, reading groups), by **number** (houses on the street, clothing sizes, hotel rooms, seats in a theater or stadium, I.D. number of students), by **name** (parts of a computer, features on our bodies, names of states within a country), or by **code** (roman numerals for chapters in a book, signs for drivers). Sometimes we combine the different systems (bones of the body may be tibia, fibula, or femur, or they may be numbered, as with vertebrae or teeth).

Closure - Discussion for Insight
What is the advantage of differentiation by color (instant recognition, as in traffic lights)? By number (infinite and can be ordered)? Ask why they have a student lunch number instead of being told their number is teal blue or navy. They will begin to see that differentiation is a cognitive decision made to create order and mastery of information.

Page 2

Things to Consider
This is where you review the elements of a plan (*Organization of Dots*)

Distinguish one part from the whole

Find the part in the midst of chaos

Work on the Sheet
Ask the students to tell you if the page begins with a part or whole (part is the answer). Can they visually memorize the shape or do they need to describe and label it ("I'm looking for a square that is about ¼ inch on each side.")?

Closure - Discussion for Insight
Can we find the one task or thing in the midst of everything going on around us? Can you focus on an assignment when there is loud noise coming from the classroom next door?

Page 3

Things to Consider
This is the same task found on page two but you need to find more than one identical part within the whole. Students will have to develop new strategies to do this.

Work on the Sheet
Ask why this task is so much more difficult than page two? Finding a shape is easier than telling how many of that shape are in the whole. It requires much closer examination. A problem will arise on page two. If we insist on the exact shape, we will probably disagree on how many copies there are. Printing variations make it difficult to agree.

Closure - Discussion for Insight
When does it matter if something is exactly the same shape or "more or less" the same shape?

Page 4

Things to Consider
The task on this page is the same task found on pages two and three - find a figure within the whole. But on this page the task looks quite different. Instead of doing one problem at a time, there are 10 simultaneous tasks. It is likely that students will skip around, perhaps doing shape seven first because it jumps out at them.

Work on the Sheet
Have students complete the task.

Closure - Discussion for Insight
When does the order of our work matter? Think of a math test. If we don't work in order, how do we make sure we haven't missed a problem?

Page 5

Things to Consider
This page is similar to page four, except it is an error page. Notice that the instructions say, "See that they are numbered correctly."

Work on the Sheet
Ask students to read the instructions. Many will interpret that to ask, "See IF they are numbered correctly." This is a chance to see how one part in a set of instructions can shape the whole task.

Closure - Discussion for Insight
Ask students to tell you what is wrong with each error. In *Comparisons* they became skilled at naming attributes such as size, shape, color, etc. This is good practice to require students to say precisely why a given answer is wrong.

Page 6

Things to Consider
Given a whole, with its component parts, can you identify the SET of parts that will exactly make up that whole?

This is a multiple choice task. Which set of parts belongs with the model?

Work on the Sheet
Ask, how many parts does the model have in it? How did you go about deciding which one was the right answer? Did you discount any frames based on the number of parts? If the model has all right angles, did they discount all answer with non-right angles? If the model has no curves, were they able to ignore all answers with curved figures, etc.?

Closure - Discussion for Insight
Can you identify things that have a defined set of parts? For example, in baseball (pitcher, catcher, etc.) or on basketball teams (guard, forward, or center).

Page 7

Things to Consider
Given a whole, with its component parts, can you identify the SET of parts that will exactly make up that whole?

This is a multiple choice task and is very similar to page six. However, the model becomes more complex in number and curved figures.

Work on the Sheet
Ask how they found the frame with the correct parts? Possibly put their strategies on the board.

Closure - Discussion for Insight
Things in life are made up of many parts working together. For example, a story has many parts (characters, plot, and setting). Our school schedule has many parts (music, physical education, art, etc.) at many grade levels.

Page 8

Things to Consider
Identify specific parts using relevant cues or salient attributes. There are six models and six sets of parts. The students will probably work in random order, quickly find the obvious answers, and take more time to compare fine details in order to solve the last few.

Work on the Sheet
Do the first one together.

Closure - Discussion for Insight
Where else do we have to look for cues (clues)? For example, when you are talking about the salient attributes of mammals, you have to know characteristics such as: have fur/hair, live birth, lower jaw made of a single bone, endothermic, etc.

Page 9

Things to Consider
Same thought as on page eight.

There are six models and six sets of parts, so now the students will probably work in random order, quickly find the obvious answers, and take more time to compare fine details in order to solve the last few.

Work on the Sheet
Have the student work on the sheet.

Closure - Discussion for Insight
Emphasis on how we decide to think makes this page valuable. Which specific thinking skills can be bridged to real life examples? For instance, how do we analyze a bike that is broken?

Page 10

Things to Consider
This is an error page. Students have to determine how to fix the error. They have to look at the model and its component parts and determine to do one of three things: add a part, remove a part, or alter a part.

Work on the Sheet
Do the first frame together.

Closure - Discussion for Insight
Discuss how to fix things by adding, subtracting or reshaping/altering. Think of a math problem that is incorrect. Do you start over? Erase just the wrong part? This page also offers the opportunity to have students articulate verbally what they see (perceive) and how they label the parts.

Page 11

Things to Consider
Can you so clearly understand a whole with all of its parts that you can look at a partial drawing and complete it so that it is identical to the original?

Notice that you have to turn the page sideways. This may not be obvious to kids.

This is the beginning of using reference points.

Work on the Sheet
Lead students to see that we begin with the whole, and we study it, and we describe it verbally. For example, the first model on this page is a bisected square with a diagonal in each half. Describing this model should help the visual process in completing the partial drawing.

Ask them where they think they'll begin drawing these shapes. Talk about reference/anchor points.

Closure - Discussion for Insight
Ask them if they can finish a task like setting the table. They can do the task if they have a model in their head as to what the finished task looks like.

Page 12

Things to Consider
This is the same task found on page 11 but is more difficult due to the lack of cues as to where a line ends, turns, or curves.

We have to create our own reference points.

Find complimentary parts to complete the whole.

Work on the Sheet
Again ask students where they would begin and talk about reference points.

Closure - Discussion for Insight
Can you finish answering the open ended math question? Yes, but only if you look at the relevant parts/model and then see what is left to do. Can you take over the presidency of the school student council and also finish the arrangements for the school talent show? Yes, but only if you compare what has already been done (part) to what needs to be done (which is the whole).

Page 13

Things to Consider
Given the whole, can you find two complementary sets of parts that together will complete that defined whole?

You can emphasize focus on the next few pages. Learners must remember to hold within their minds the model shape (the whole) and two additional drawings, combine the two visually and determine whether together they make **more** than the model, **less** than the model, or **exactly** the model.

Work on the Sheet
Have students work on the page. Discussion will be interesting. Some may start with a numbered partial drawing and imagine what else they will add to complete the model. Only then will they look at the lettered options to find the drawing in their heads. Other students may use visual transport to combine two partial drawings. Then they will compare the results to the model. Some may use a subtraction process, subtracting the numbered drawing from the model and finding the result on the lettered side.

Closure - Discussion for Insight
Taking time for discussion about the above activity is key here. Discuss the three strategies (additive, subtractive or equivalent) to re-create the model.

Page 14

Things to Consider
Same as page 13 but with increasing complexity.

Work on the Sheet
Same as before.

Closure - Discussion for Insight
Talk about the difference between this page and page 13. The task becomes increasingly more complex (more abstract, more parts, and more details).

Page 15

Things to Consider
Same as page 14. However, it is more complex with curved figures.

Work on the Sheet
Same as page 14.

Closure - Discussion for Insight
Same as page 14.

Page 16

Things to Consider
Same as page 15, though it is an error page.

Work on the Sheet
Same as page 14.

Closure - Discussion for Insight
To fix something that is broken such as a clock, you need to analyze how it works before putting it back together.

To construct something such as a play, you have to know the parts. In a story, you have to know the parts of a story (characters, plot, setting, etc.).

Page 17

Things to Consider
Same as page 15 though it is more visually complex.

Work on the Sheet
Same as page 15.

Closure - Discussion for Insight
If you get to the last one on the page and discover that it is not right, what can you conclude? You may conclude that there is another error on the page.

Page 18

Things to Consider
Given a whole, with its parts, can you look at a new whole and determine what parts of the model were combined to make this new completed whole?

On the top half of the page, the blue dot that uses all of the numbered parts is the new single whole.

This unit also requires students to use a code to indicate which parts are utilized to make the new whole.

Work on the Sheet
Discuss with students that orientation/rotation matters. There is no rotation of the new whole; students must maintain the original orientation of the wholes and parts. Shape, size and direction are attributes that must be simultaneously held in the learners' minds.

Closure - Discussion for Insight
This is great practice for solving complex problems whose parts are interrelated.

Page 19

Things to Consider
Same as on page 18. Again, orientation matters.

Work on the Sheet
Label (encode) them in order. This is good practice for students who always want to "start over" instead of "fixing up" things that are not quite accurate.

Closure - Discussion for Insight
The parts are now a new whole. For example, when you mix yellow and blue you get green.

Page 20

Things to Consider
Same as on page 19 but is an error page.

Orientation and number matter but color does not.

Work on the Sheet
Have students work on the sheet.

Closure - Discussion for Insight
You must discuss the nature of the error.

Page 21

Things to Consider
Can you understand a part (actually a whole in itself) so clearly that you can locate it and record (color in) its location in a larger, more complex whole?

Remember to have the students turn the page sideways before beginning the work.

Work on the Sheet
Ask the students what they notice. This task is similar to unit one where color is a distractor. It forces the learner to disregard something that is bold and obvious in order to focus on that which is relevant to the task. The problems have many details and students are required to pay precise attention to them.

Closure - Discussion for Insight
Many complex problems can be solved if the main difficulty can be isolated.

Page 22

Things to Consider
Same as on page 21.

Work on the Sheet
Same as page 21.

Closure - Discussion for Insight
Sometimes our desire for completion is stronger than our desire to follow the rules.

Page 23

Things to Consider
Can you so clearly understand a whole (goal) with its component parts, that you can then take just some of those parts and construct a new whole from them?

This unit requires a construction task, something much harder to do generally than completing a description task. Remember, construction is always harder than destruction.

Use reference points.

Work on the Sheet
Have students think of a pantry filled with food. Imagine that you take just some items (such as flour, sugar, raisins, butter, and salt) and construct something new, cookies, using just those component parts. Notice the instructions; you are to construct a new single whole, with NO internal lines. In other words, the individual parts are no longer seen as discreet; for they have been unified with the other parts to make that single shape.

Closure - Discussion for Insight
Organizing (synthesizing) parts into meaningful wholes (combining) is a valuable skill to cultivate. However, we need to be aware of what the final result will be. For example, having a successful school day means that we must combine going to class with chores and playing.

Page 24

Things to Consider
Same as page 23, however, it is more complex and requires more reference points.

Work on the Sheet
Same as on page 23.

Closure - Discussion for Insight
Where else do you need to use reference points?

Page 25

Things to Consider
Construction is harder than destruction.

Given a whole made up of parts, can you construct a new single whole according to a formula?

Work on the Sheet
Ask what is different on this page (curved shapes). Use reference points and complete the page.

Closure - Discussion for Insight
Ask students which is harder, construction or destruction? Why?

www.ingramcontent.com/pod-product-compliance
Lightning Source LLC
Chambersburg PA
CBHW021003230426
43666CB00005B/261